SCHIRMER'S LIBRARY OF MUSICAL CLASSICS

Vol. 227

FELIX MENDELSSOHN-BARTHOLDY

Organ Works

THREE PRELUDES AND FUGUES
Op. 37

SIX SONATAS
Op. 65

STUDENTS' EDITION

Edited and Fingered by

SAMUEL P. WARREN

G. SCHIRMER, Inc.

DISTRIBUTED BY

HAL•LEONARD®
CORPORATION

7777 W. BLUEMOUND RD. P.O. BOX 13819 MILWAUKEE, WI 53213

PREFATORY REMARKS

BY THE COMPOSER.

In these Sonatas much depends upon a proper selection of the organ-stops. As every organ with which I am acquainted, however, requires its own mode of treatment—stops of the same name in different instruments not always producing a like effect—I have indicated, in a general way, only the kind of effect required, without specifying names of stops. By *fortissimo,* I intend the full organ ; by *pianissimo,* generally a soft eight-foot stop alone ; by *forte,* the great organ without some of the loudest stops ; by *piano,* several soft eight-foot stops combined, and so forth. In the pedal I desire, throughout, even in *pianissimo,* eight- and sixteen-foot tone together, except where the contrary is expressly stated (see the Sixth Sonata). It is, therefore, left to the organist to make such combinations as are appropriate to the various movements, but he should take care, when employing two manuals, that they differ in tone-color, without, at the same time, standing out in too great contrast.

NOTE BY THE EDITOR.—With reference to the above prefatory remarks, the editor desires to have it understood that such extra indications in registration as he has given are to be regarded simply as suggestions They are not intended in the slightest degree to forestall the general directions of the composer, but rather to aid the student in more readily carrying these out.

CONTENTS

Three Preludes and Fugues
for the Organ.

(Dedicated to Thomas Attwood, of London.)

F. MENDELSSOHN. Op. 37.
Composed 1837.

Prelude, No. 1.

∧ = Right Toe.
∨ = Left Toe.
▢ = Right Heel.
⊔ = Left Heel.

Gt. 16′ & 4′ Foundation stops.
Sw. Full coupled to Gt.
Ped. 16′ & 8′; coup. to Gt.

12572 *) The metronome numbers to the three preludes and fugues are suggested by the Editor.

Sw. Soft 8' with light Reed.
Ch. Dulciana&Flute 8'.
Ped. 16' & 8'.

Prelude, Nº 2.

Fugue, Nº 2.

Gt. & Sw. Diapasons & Flutes 8´.
Sw. 16´ & 8´ with couplers.
Ped. 16´ & 8´, with Gt. Coupler.

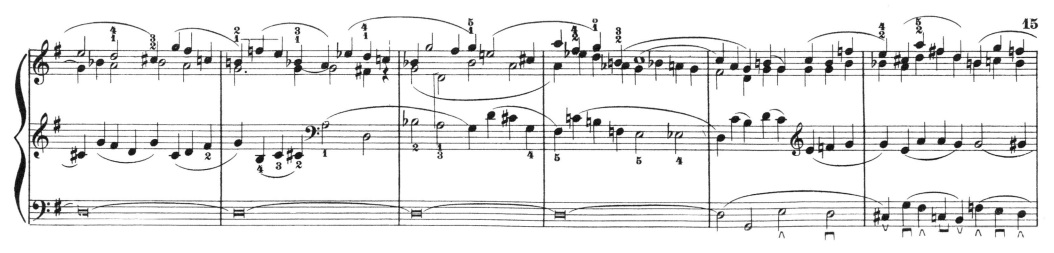

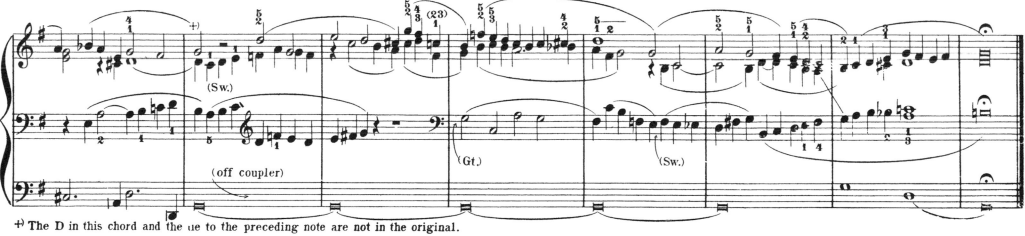

+) The D in this chord and the tie to the preceding note are not in the original.

Gt. Full without reeds.
Sw. Full coupled to Gt.
Ped. 16′ & 8′; Gt. coupler.

Prelude, Nº 3.

Allegro. (♩ = 69)

(Mixtures.)

(Sw.)

(Gt.: off Mixtures.)

(Gt.)

(Mixtures.)

Fugue, No. 3.

Full Organ. (♩ = 66)

Six Sonatas
for the Organ.
Dedicated to Dr. F. Schlemmer of Frankfort on the Main.
Sonata, № 1.

∧ = Right Toe.
∨ = Left Toe.
⊓ = Right Heel.
⊔ = Left Heel.

Gt. Full, without reeds.
Sw. Full coupled to Gt.
Ped. Full without reeds; Gt. coupler.

F. MENDELSSOHN. Op. 65.
1844−45

Allegro moderato, e serioso. ($\bullet$ = 92)

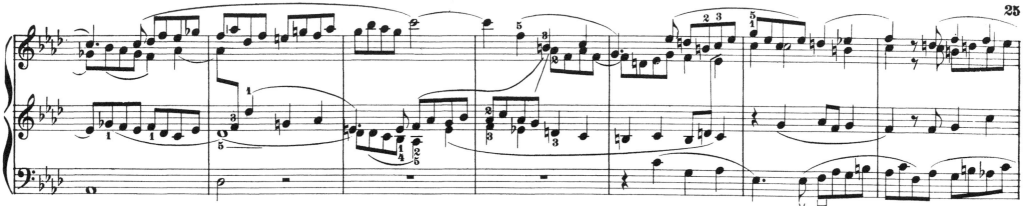

(Mixtures.)

Man. II.
mezzo p (Sw. Diaps., soft 8' Reed ad lib.)

a) These four measures read thus in the original:

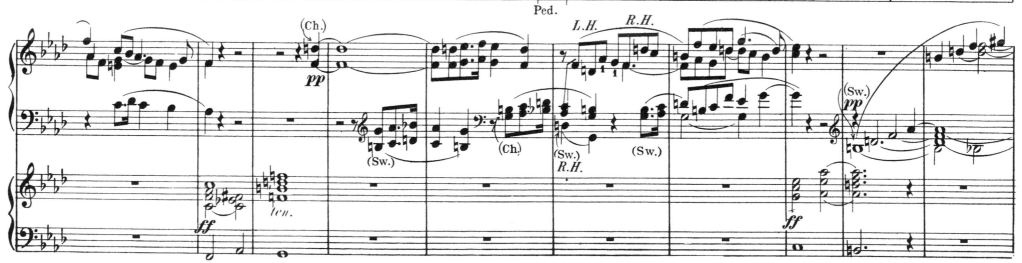

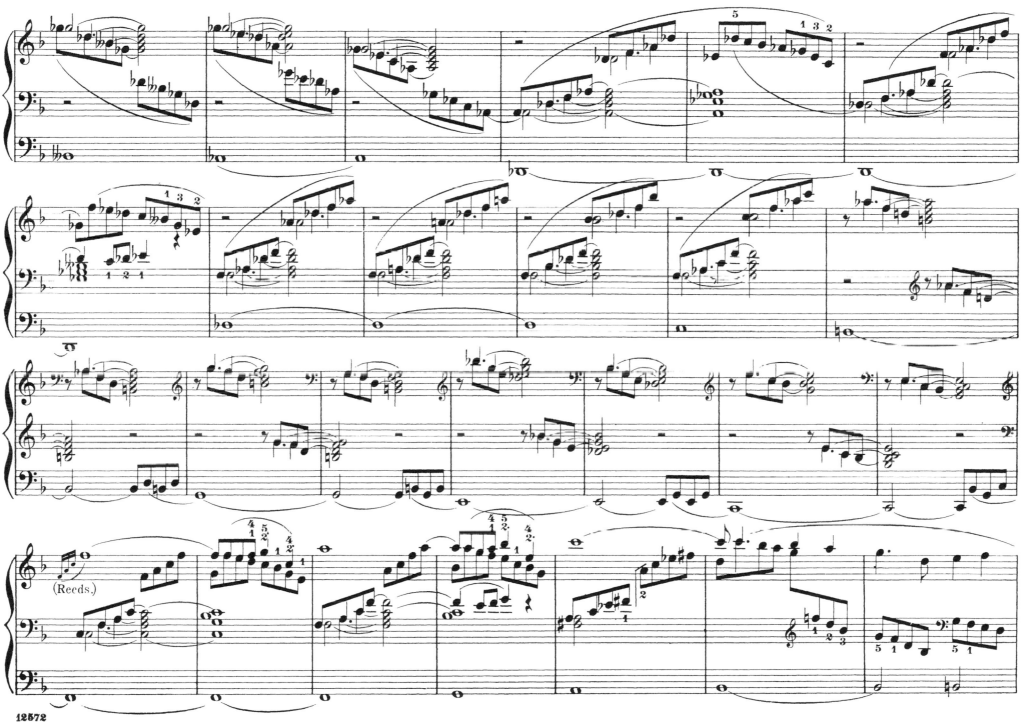

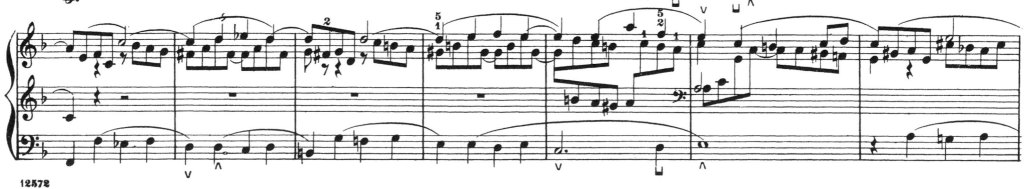

(Full Org.)

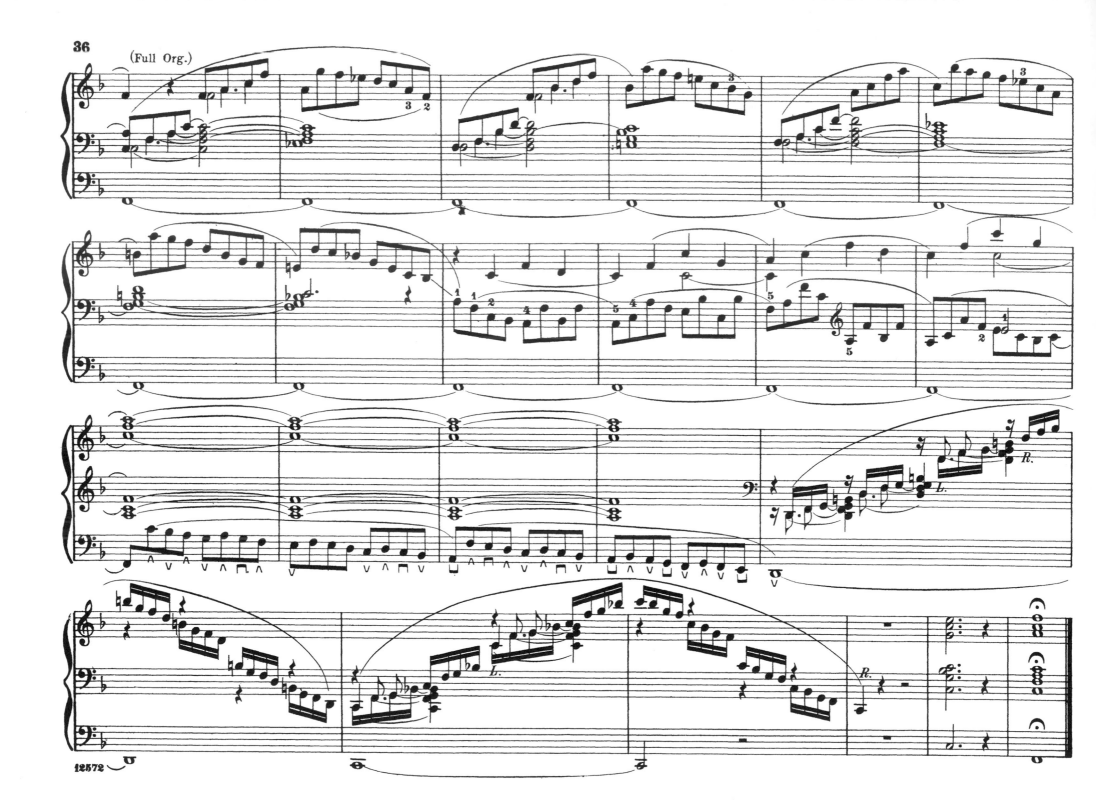

Sonata, Nº 2.

Gt. 8′ Foundation stops coupled to Sw.
Sw. 8′ & 4′   ″   ″   with Oboe.
Ped. 16′ & 8′ Gt. Coupler.

Grave. ($\quad$= 69.)

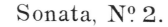

Manuals.

Pedal.

12572

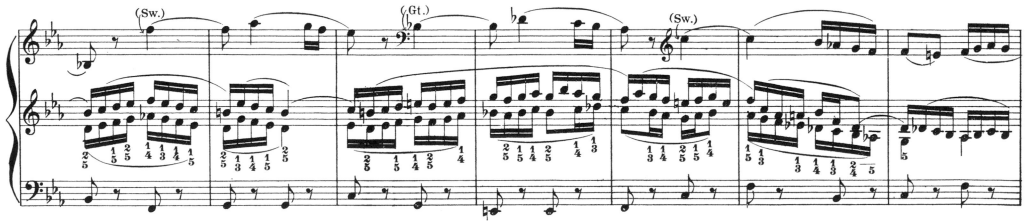

Gt. 16; 8' & 4' ft. with full Sw.
Ped. to balance.

Allegro maestoso e vivace.
(♩ = 92.)

attacca la Fuga

Gt. 8′ & 4′; with Sw. full.
Ch. full with Sw.
Ped. 16′ & 8′; with Couplers.

Fuga.

Allegro moderato. (♩=132.)

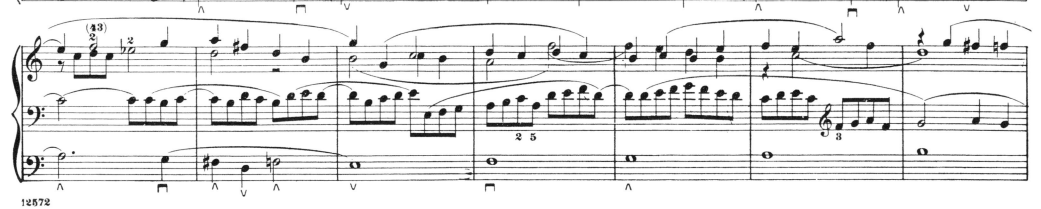

Gt. & Sw. full coupled.
Ch. full, with Sw.
Ped. full, with coupler to Gt.

Sonata № 3.

12572

CHORAL.("In deepest need I cry to Thee.")

da questa parte fino al maggiore poco a poco più animato e più forte (sino al ♩ = 100).

(Sw. or Ch. with Sw.)

(Gt.)

(Gt.)

Gt. 8′ & 4′ foundation Stops.
Sw. full, coupled to Gt.
Ped. to balance—16′ & 8′, coupled to Gt.

Sonata, № 4.

Allegro con brio. (♩ = 100.)

Manuals.

Pedal.

(Mixtures.)

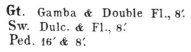

58

Sw. St. Diap. and Oboe.
Ch. Dulc. or Viol da Gamba 8', with soft Fl. 8'.
Gt. Double Fl. 8', — Swell coupler.

12572

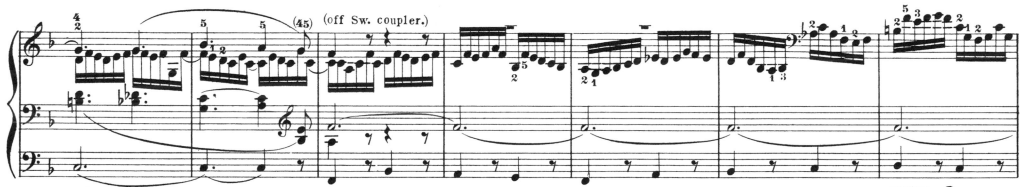

(off Sw. coupler.)

(Sw.)

(pp)

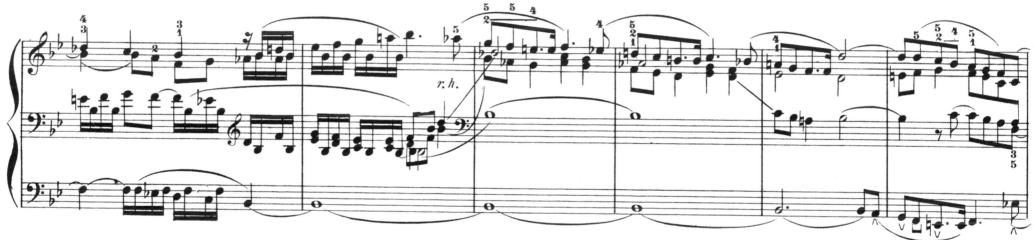

Sonata, Nº 5.

attacca.

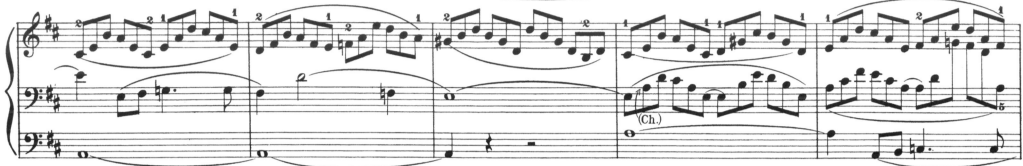

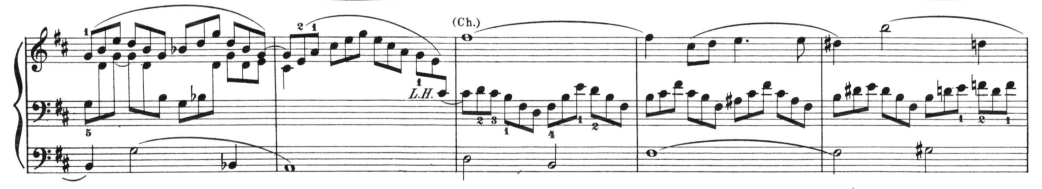

Gt. & Sw. 8′ with light 16′.
Ped. 16′ & 8′, with Gt. coupler.

Sonata, № 6.

"Our Father who art in Heaven"—
„Vater unser im Himmelreich."

Man. I.
(Sw. or Ch. Flutes 8' & 4'.)

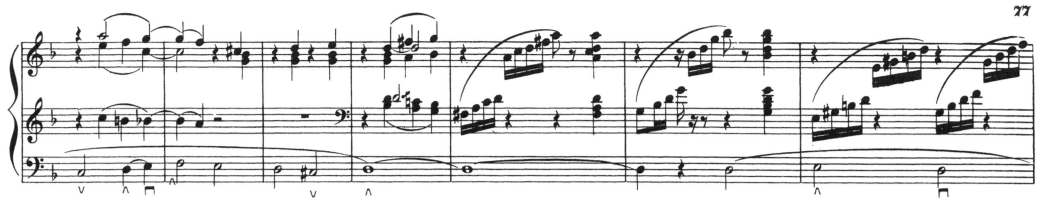

attacca la Fuga.

Fuga.

Gt. 8' & 4'
Sw. 16', 8' & 4' } Coupled.
Ped. 16' & 8', & Coupler Gt.

Sostenuto e legato. (♩ = 96.)

Sw. Diapasons 8'.
Ch. Dul. & Fl. 8'.
Ped. Gamba 16' & Fl. 8'.

Finale.

Andante. ($\bullet$ = 100.)

p e dolce.

p e dolce.